IMAGES
of America

THE WHITE MOUNTAINS OF APACHE COUNTY

The White Mountain Historical Society is committed to preserving the history of the Springerville-Eagar area. Sandstone markers, placed in front of historic buildings, form the Pistols, Plows, and Petticoats tour. These historic buildings were moved to create the White Mountain Historical Park, shown here in Springerville's winter snow. (Photograph by Roxanne Knight.)

ON THE COVER: White Mountain pastures are used to fatten cattle during the summer. The Apache County seal features a classic Hereford bull and the year of the county formation, 1879. Herefords were brought in to upgrade early cattle herds, although many ranchers prefer a polled (hornless) strain. (ACHS/St. Johns.)

IMAGES
of America

THE WHITE MOUNTAINS OF APACHE COUNTY

Catherine H. Ellis and D. L. Turner

ARCADIA
PUBLISHING

Published by Arcadia Publishing
Charleston, South Carolina

Library of Congress Control Number: 2009937658

For all general information contact Arcadia Publishing at:
Telephone 843-853-2070
Fax 843-853-0044
E-mail sales@arcadiapublishing.com
For customer service and orders:
Toll-Free 1-888-313-2665

Visit us on the Internet at www.arcadiapublishing.com

*To the men and women who have worked to
preserve the history of Apache County*

CONTENTS

In Memoriam

Fidencio A. Baca (1930–2009) and Jack A. Becker (1942–2007)

Fidencio "Fide" Baca recently wrote, "I first became interested in history at the age of 10, when I accompanied my parents on a pilgrimage to Zuni Pueblo in New Mexico to see the *Santo Niño*. The *Santo Niño* is a statue of the Christ Child that was brought to Zuni Pueblo from Spain by the Franciscan monks in 1629, when they built the Franciscan Mission Church in Zuni. In 1680, when all of the Pueblo Indians of New Mexico rebelled against the Spaniards, the Kanesta family, who had been converted to the Catholic Church, hid the statue and the priests' vestments. Today, 329 years later, you can visit the statue at the house of the descendents of the Kanesta family in Zuni. About 20 years ago, the Diocese of Gallup and the Zuni Catholic people built a new chapel at the site of the old Mission." An interest in history defined Fide's life, and he generously shared his notebooks and photographs with anyone interested.

Jack Becker was a lifelong resident of Round Valley who spent most of his spare time researching official records and old newspapers in order to document and better understand Springerville's early history. In 1992, he stated, "The Round Valley is a really rich multi-cultural mosaic of many elements, each of which has played a very important role in bringing us where we are today." The research of both Baca and Becker greatly enhanced this book.

ACKNOWLEDGMENTS

Clarcia Eagar wrote a short history of Round Valley and stated, "I have made no attempt to name all of the early settlers, nor to include a balanced account of all events. I have written about what I know best. Even after research, I have not always been able to determine which version of a story is true. The earliest history is not recorded; much has been lost, and I'm not sure that I have not overlooked some existing history." Although Clarcia Eagar's disclaimer could also be applied to this book, we hope our selection of images and stories is broad enough to be representative of the area and enjoyed by all.

Sincere thanks go to the many people who have written about Apache County history or who helped us gather information, especially Fidencio Baca, Jack Becker, Wink Crigler, George Crosby, Clarcia Eagar, JoAnn Hatch, Blanche and Merrell Hamblin, John Ray Hamblin, Christine Marin, E. Widtsoe Shumway, LeRoy "Roy" and Mabel Wilhelm, and Milo Wiltbank. Dewey and Esther Farr collected photographs and artifacts now at the Apache County Historical Society. Jared Jackson at Arcadia Publishing was essential to the project.

Sources for the photographs are noted in parentheses at the end of each caption. We are grateful to all who shared with us. We also used images from the following institutions: the Arizona Historical Society at Tucson (AHS/Tucson); the Center for Southwest Research, University Libraries, University of New Mexico (CSWR/New Mexico); the Family History Center at St. Johns (FHC/St. Johns); the Apache County Historical Society (ACHS/St. Johns); the Apache-Sitgreaves National Forests (Apache-Sitgreaves); and the White Mountain Historical Society in Springerville-Eagar (WMHS).

Finally, although the title of this book is *The White Mountains of Apache County*, lines dividing counties and states often do not make sense in a historic context. We have included a few photographs from Greenlee County and New Mexico because these areas are part of the White Mountains, while McNary, although briefly mentioned here, should really be discussed in connection with Navajo County.

Escudilla Mountain (above in 1938) dominates the landscape in southern Apache County. Its slopes are covered with towering ponderosa pine, and spruce grace the higher elevations. The Spaniards named it Escudilla because it resembled the metal bowl or cup used for food and water. Escudilla is only one of many White Mountain peaks that are the source of major Arizona rivers, including the Salt (fed by the Black and White Rivers), the Little Colorado (below), and the San Francisco (tributaries Blue River and Eagle Creek). (Above, photograph by Max Hunt; below, Apache-Sitgreaves.)

INTRODUCTION

The mountains in today's southern Apache County were called Sierra Blanca (White Mountains) by early Spanish and Hispanic explorers. Here the new grass of spring melds into summer flowers, and the gold of aspen leaves fades under winter snow. Flowing north from the White Mountains is the Little Colorado River called To Chaco by the Navajos and Rio Colorado Chiquito by the Spaniards. Its waters have been used to irrigate the land since pioneer times. In 1877, six-year-old Joseph "Joe" Pearce traveled with his family from Utah to Arizona and settled in the western White Mountains around Taylor and Heber. He later wrote, "The forest was alive with game. The streams ran full of trout . . . the turkey came down within a mile of our ranch at Taylor. . . . The forest was thick with deer, every kind, black-tail, mule, white-tail." He also noted antelope, mountain lions, and mountain sheep. The White Mountains were also home to Merriam's elk, a subspecies that was hunted to extinction by about 1895.

Pearce remembered growing up in a "raw county, with toughs for my friends and toughs for my enemies, and never sure which a man was." He described learning to shoot a six-gun at age 14, and that "I was really getting ready to be an outlaw or a law man, and in the West . . . there wasn't often much more than a hairline of difference between the two." Cattle rustling and outlaw activities were particularly bad in Apache County, where Pearce lived as an adult. He, however, turned to law enforcement and served as a Forest Service ranger, an Arizona Ranger under Capt. Thomas Rynning, a line rider for the Apache Whiteriver Indian Reservation, a special county ranger for Apache County, and a livestock detective for the State Livestock Sanitary Board. By 1910, most outlaw activity had ceased. Pearce's comments on some of the early residents of Apache County included the Slaughter boys, who "worked their dad's outfit on Black River." Pearce commented, "They were just lively boys. . . . They wore their hair long and packed guns and liked to think of themselves as bad men when they really weren't."

In 1909, much of the forest acreage in the White Mountains was designated a U.S. National Forest. Forest Rangers came in to regulate logging and grazing. Pearce wrote that the rangers had to mark trees for logging operations and estimate the number of board feet. "Each tree to be cut had to have two notches, one above the cut and one that would remain on the stump. In the mill, each log had to have a U.S. cut into it, and I had to estimate the number of board feet in each log and make a report of how many board feet had been cut."

The friction between ranchers who had previously pastured cattle freely and Forest Service Rangers who wanted to limit cattle to prevent overgrazing was noted by forest supervisor Kenner Kartchner. He described meeting with ranchers in New Mexico and wrote, "Our proposals went over rather lukewarm, but at the close we were invited to a dance up the canyon, which had been planned to coincide with the meeting." Kartchner, a noted fiddler in northern Arizona, but unknown in New Mexico, volunteered to relieve, or "spell off," the fiddler, Mrs. Jack Young. Kartchner recalled that "the hush that fell over the crowd, especially ranchers we had met with that afternoon, bespoke their utter astonishment at the thoughts of such a thing." When he began "Leather Breeches," a familiar Texas hoedown, the crowd was first stunned and then "whooped and hollered, stomped and laughed." Kartchner observed, "Almost to a man, those present at the afternoon meeting gathered around to shake hands, congratulate, ask where I was from, and express amazement at the combination of a deputy forest supervisor and country fiddler. We had reached a hearty common ground that I enjoyed as much as they." When the dance was over, Kartchner's companion, O. L. Coleman, "remarked that our meeting would have been far more successful had the dance been held first."

Since Henry Ford's time, the mountains have attracted visitors from across the state and nation. The towns of Springerville and Eagar, also known as Round Valley, are often called the "Gateway to the White Mountains." In 1913, the Good Roads Association published a series of Arizona maps that stated, "The towns of Springerville and Eager [sic], in eastern Arizona, situated as they are on the natural automobile route from coast to coast, will be found an oasis to the weary traveler, where he can find hotel accomodations [sic] and supplies suited for his immediate needs, adjacent to and the outfitting point for the great hunting and fishing regions of the beautiful white mountains."

Early automobile pathfinder Anthon L. Westgard's first trip through the White Mountains was in November 1910. On his second trip in April 1911, he encountered poor roads around Springerville. When traveling west, his party spent eight days covering 42 miles. Westgard wrote, "We do not measure stretches between towns by distance any longer, but by time." In November of that year, he was guide for a caravan of Garford cars with paying tourists sponsored by the American Automobile Association (AAA) and the Raymond and Whitcomb Company. When they reached the White Mountains this time, the cars sank to their hubs in the mud, then "the mercury sank also, down to zero." The men spent 12 hours jacking up the cars and placing logs under the wheels for mile after mile.

Automobile travel was primitive and difficult when trying to keep a schedule. For residents, however, excursions were easier because travel could simply be taken when the weather was good. On August 5, 1913, Gustav and Louise Becker of Springerville, Naomi and Olga Becker of New Orleans, and Lydia Franz of Clifton traveled to Fort Apache and, stopping at Corydon Cooley's ranch house, signed his guest book. Both Cooley's guest book and Becker's garage register show regular "coast to coast" visitors after 1910. Westgard thought that Arizona should encourage tourism more and wrote, "I have for years traveled through their territory, [and] have written widely of the wonderful attractions, scenically, archaeologically, and otherwise." Then he noted that Springerville (undoubtedly through the efforts of Gustav Becker) was the most appreciative of his services.

A native son and beloved cowboy poet of the White Mountains, Milo Wiltbank wrote exclusively of this area. Both his life and his poetry bridged the outlaw/cowboy era and the summer visitor use of the ponderosa forest. His poem "Round Valley Rodeo" invites all to enjoy the mountains in Apache County:

Up in the hills where the bull is king
And fancy clothes don't mean a thing
Where women wear Levis and buckskin vests
And the men grow horse hair upon their chests.

Now come up early for there's plenty to do
Everybody will welcome you
You can fish or loaf or camp in the shade
Till the show starts off with the big parade.

Up in the hills where the cow is queen
Where the good cool air is fresh and clean
'Neath the timbered hills where tall pines grow
Come meet your friends at the rodeo.

One

EL VALLE REDONDO

Aside from Native Americans already residing in the area, settlement of the White Mountains in Arizona began with Hispanic families from the Rio Grande valley. Juan Baca traveled through *el valle redondo* about 1870. Early Hispanic families included the Apodaca, Aragon, Bustamante, Candelaria, Castillo, Chavez, Carillo, Cordova, Cruz, Gallegos, Jaramillo, Lujan, Mascareño, Peña, Padilla, Romero, Sanchez, Savedra, Silva, Tafoya, and Vijil families. Other men were married to Hispanic women, including St. George Creaghe, Henry Springer, William Milligan, Oren McCullough, and Anthony Long. As Fidencio Baca wrote, "When the Spanish settlers first arrived in Valle Redondo (Round Valley), they brought their faith with them—the Roman Catholic faith. No Catholic priest accompanied them . . . the nearest Catholic churches were in Socorro and Luna, New Mexico. [They] kept their faith by gathering in different homes for velorios [all-night vigils], rosarios, and the reenactment of the posadas."

The history of southern Apache County can be told in the names of its towns. Greer is named after an early family from Texas. Eagar (spelled with two *a*'s) recognizes Mormon brothers John, Joel, and William Eagar. The largest town, Springerville, was named after Henry Springer from Albuquerque, who established a large store in the fall of 1875. He contracted to purchase all the grain that could be grown, and the *Arizona Citizen* reported, "Every man, woman, and child is busy taking out new ditches and enlarging old ones, preparatory to planting a very large crop, perhaps double the amount of last year." Springer, however, went broke. The *Weekly Arizona Miner* noted in 1877, "We believe Mr. Springer's present embarrassment is caused by having several thousand dollars tied up in barley, at Springerville in this country, which he has been unable to dispose of. We hope he will come out all right." Springer returned to Albuquerque and left nothing but his name for the town.

Solitary trappers seeking beaver pelts traveled throughout the Intermountain West in the early 19th century. In Arizona, Sylvester and James "Ohio" Pattie, father and son, trapped along the San Francisco, Gila, and San Pedro Rivers in 1825–1826. James left an exaggerated account of their travels. Juan Baca, an early settler of Round Valley, was a beaver trapper. (Engraving by W. M. Cary, *Harper's Weekly*, September 9, 1876.)

Earlier residents were from the Anasazi and Mogollon cultures. Their presence, particularly north of Springerville, was evident in the amount of pottery excavated from the area. Manufacture of pottery began about 200 AD and was used to store valuable seed grain, preserving it from mold and insects. These specimens were acquired by Sol Barth and Reamer Ling; most were later donated to museums. (FHC/St. Johns.)

Albert Franklin Banta (at right, in 1918), an expert hunter and trapper, was an early guide for the U.S. Army. He wrote, "At this time I wore a full buckskin suit with a fox-skin cap with the tail hanging. Of course I was a foolsight to see, but at that time did not realize what an ass I was or how ridiculous I looked." In 1870, a 24-year-old Banta, or Charles Franklin as he was known then, was freighting between Zuni (below) and Prescott. On one trip, he discovered Meteor Crater (initially called Franklin's Folly). He helped settle Apache County, established a newspaper at St. Johns in 1882, and was elected district attorney in 1889. Banta wrote, "I have followed almost every occupation under the sun, from bull-whacking and mule-skinning down to politics, with one notable exception, stage robbing." (Both ACHS/St. Johns.)

Eliza Rudd came to Round Valley in 1876. She remembered that "at first there was nothing much to fear except Indians, and there was no trouble with them for three or four years. Friendly Indians sometimes passed with their families on a hunting trip. Once they camped near our ranch. The chief came in and talked to us. They camped close for a week. Again we heard that Geronimo was coming, but he came no closer than Alpine." The White Mountain Apaches were mostly peaceful. Supplying grain to Fort Apache (above), however, was the reason that settlers came from New Mexico. A group of military men (below) are somewhere on the "Apache Trail." (Above, Ellis collection; below, CSWR/New Mexico 000-742-0679.)

Widtsoe Shumway wrote that Alpine citizens believed a "mixture of fact and fable. . . . The Alma, New Mexico massacre, and the burning of Quemado by Victorio in 1880, and the killing of approximately 1,000 whites in southern Arizona and Mexico during Geronimo's rampage, and other hit and run tactics made deep impressions on whites throughout early Arizona." The eventual outcome came after Gen. George Crook was assigned to Arizona. He used Apaches as scouts (above) and negotiated peace with Geronimo (below). Following an additional outbreak, Geronimo's band, as well as the loyal scouts, was exiled to Florida. Shumway concluded, "By 1886, the Indian ceased to be a real threat . . . but people had heard and told so many stories that for a long time they continued to be [intimidated] and were constantly on guard and suspicious." (Both CSWR/New Mexico; above, 000-742-0338, below, 000-742-0238.)

Casa Malpais, 2 miles north of Springerville, was visited by Frank Cushing (left), a young anthropologist from Washington, D.C., who spent four and a half years among the Zunis, 30 miles south of Fort Wingate. He pioneered anthropologists living with their subjects; he not only lived with the Zunis but dressed in their clothing and ate their food. This woodcut depicts Cushing as a war chief. In May 1883, he traveled to "the great elevated *malpais* plains which skirt the White Mountains and Sierra [Escudilla]" and found ruins where springs occurred. He noted the fissures where "granaries, places of refuge, worship and burial, depositories of sacrifices, implements and weapons, refuse, etc." were found. Because Casa Malpais was easily defended, it was occupied into the 14th century. Fidencio Baca (below) was instrumental in making Casa Malpais available through organized tours. (At left, *Century Illustrated Monthly Magazine*, 1882; below, Fidencio Baca.)

Banta wrote, "At this time, 1870, there was not a settlement or single soul to be met with from the time I left Zuni until I reached Bob Postle's ranch in Chino Valley, 25 miles [north] of Prescott." Supplies for Fort Apache initially came from Zuni (through St. Johns), but later most supplies came from Belen, New Mexico, through Springerville. Shown here is John Becker's mill in the 1890s. (AHS/Tucson, Becker collection.)

In 1871, C. E. Cooley guided a detachment from Camp Apache to San Marcial, New Mexico. Then William Milligan, O. W. McCullough, and Anthony Long arranged to build barracks at Camp Apache. The *Santa Fe New Mexican* of March 1871 reported, "Milligan and Long have taken up a tract of land, formed a settlement [Round Valley], and built a number of houses in which families are now living." This ruin is Fort Redondo, built by Leandro Carillo. (Trish Patterson.)

The Becker family emigrated from Germany. In 1874, Julius Becker (left) came to Round Valley, and two years later his brother Gustav (standing) followed; their brother John (right) remained in Belen. Gustav and Julius established Becker Mercantile; an old ledger from the store shows the first sale to Dionicio Baca in March 1876. (Becker/Harper collection.)

Julius and Gustav Becker married Homrighausen sisters Wilhemina "Minna" and Louise, respectively. Julius and his family all died of illness, but Gustav contributed significantly to the development of Apache County. Pictured here from left to right is the Gustav Becker family about 1906: (first row) Gustav, Emma, Hugo, Julius, Arthur, and Louise; (second row) Alvin, Edward, Lucie, and Paul. (Margie Harper.)

Half-brothers Francisco and Dionicio Baca came to Springerville from Belen, sometime between 1870 and 1877, freighting supplies to Fort Apache. They later encouraged others to settle in Arizona, including the families of Andrea Hall and Alberto Depew. Dionicio was elected Apache County treasurer in 1885 and is shown at right with Henry Huning (standing) and Corydon Cooley (seated right). Francisco married Cruz Chavez and is shown below about 1920 with grandsons Juanito (John, left) and Andrez (Andrew) Candelaria, sons of Otario and Rita Candelaria. (Both Fidencio Baca.)

Eliza Catherine Rudd (left) came to Arizona in 1876. The Rudd and Bush families left Fort Smith, Arkansas, in April with three wagons, 40 head of cattle, and six horses. Other families joined up, returned home, and/or left for different destinations. At one time, there were 21 wagons and 200 head of cattle. The travelers hunted buffalo and antelope, found wild plums, cherries, and currants, and cooked with buffalo chips, wood, and weeds. One baby was born. At Salt Lake, New Mexico, they stopped to wash and sack salt. They arrived at Round Valley August 25 and "lived in tents for about three weeks" at Water Canyon (below, unidentified campers). (At left, *Arizona Sheriff,* December 1937; below, ACHS/St. Johns.)

The Rudd family planted seed grain (mostly barley) and began building and fencing. The men made 5,000 rails the first winter. This photograph shows a typical early ranch headquarters complete with rail fence. It was located at Black River and owned by John Eagar. (ACHS/St. Johns.)

William Rudd delivered a baby for the wife of Leandro Carrillo the day after they arrived. Rudd practiced medicine in Arkansas and continued in Arizona. He also studied law and became county attorney. Eliza Rudd commented, "As the years went by, conditions began to improve. We bought our home in Springerville [above] in the fall of 1886. Springerville was growing. It had stores, a school, Sunday school, and very occasionally, church services." (Apache-Sitgreaves.)

Early freighters included the William Lund family of Nutrioso, seen above, who hauled locally produced commodities (including butter and cheese) to Magdalena, New Mexico, and then brought back supplies. The front wagon appears to be hauling cloth. A more typical freight outfit, however, is shown below, with double wagons pulled by six horses. The front wagon could carry 3,000 to 4,000 pounds and the back wagon 2,500 to 3,000. Freighting, particularly hauling supplies from the railroad to Fort Apache, sustained many pioneer families. James Jennings's list of freight included barbed wire, rock salt, flour, sugar, oats, barley, Timothy hay (from New York state), clothing, walnuts, canned goods, and cookies, particularly Uneeda Biscuit (from National Biscuit Company, now Nabisco). (Above, WMHS; below, Apache-Sitgreaves.)

When members of the Church of Jesus Christ of Latter-day Saints (Mormons) first came to northern Arizona, there was immediate friction, particularly over the practice of polygamy. Original settlers saw polygamy as immoral and unlawful. Many Mormons thought a polygamous marriage in Utah would not be prosecuted in Arizona—they were wrong. Of the three Eagar brothers (above, from left to right, Joel, William, and John), Joel and John were polygamists and soon moved to Mexico. George Crosby (below, left) served eight months in the Yuma Penitentiary, but when he returned to Utah in 1899, his wife Sarah (below, right) divorced him and stayed in Arizona. Peter J. Christofferson of Springerville saw himself as "a prisoner for conscience sake" when he was in prison in Detroit, Michigan. In 1890, Wilford Woodruff, president of the LDS Church, issued "the Manifesto," which ended new polygamous marriages. (Above, Keith Eagar; below, FHC/St. Johns.)

In June 1876, with a letter from Springerville, Yavapai County, Arizona Territory, the *Weekly Arizona Miner* reported, "There are perhaps between 200 and 800 Mormons settled upon the Rio Colorado Chiquito. They will plow about 1,000 acres this year, and have already set out nearly 20 acres of fruit trees. The 'head men of the tribe' say they will put up a steam saw-mill and grist-mill this fall. I should judge from the way the Mormons have started in, they intend to 'stick,' and to make permanent homes in Arizona." Two early Mormon families were the Ellis T. Wiltbank family, pictured above at Greer with family friend Margaret Jarvis Overton and children in the doorway, and the Hiram Bigelow family at left. Bigelow's gristmill was used by all, free of charge. (Above, ACHS/St. Johns; below, Iris Finch.)

Jacob Hamblin, pictured with his wife, Priscilla, lived his entire life on the frontier. Born in 1819, he first lived in Ohio and Wisconsin before moving on to Illinois and Utah. He became a peacemaker with the Gosiute, Shoshoni, and Paiute. He was asked to lead a delegation to visit the Navajo and Moqui (Hopi) in 1858, and in 1878, he moved to Arizona. He passed away in 1886 and is buried at Alpine. (FHC/St. Johns.)

Of July 3, 1892, Jesse N. Smith, Snowflake Stake president, wrote, "The morning light revealed a great encampment of Saints scattered among the trees of the beautiful pine forest" at Pinetop. Representatives from Maricopa (Mesa), St. Joseph (Thatcher), St. Johns, and Snowflake Stakes attended (Smith reported 1,152 people). There were speeches and a dance and several weddings, including the wedding of Waity Slade and Benjamin Crosby, pictured here. (LaVerl Crosby.)

The Becker brothers' farming and mercantile business grew. About 1880, they purchased the store above (shown around 1895) and made improvements through the years. Gustav Becker's sons contributed greatly to the community: Julius operated the store and promoted good roads, Paul ran Valley National Bank, and Alvin developed Round Valley Light and Power. Gus also had cattle at the Jokake Ranch, which was operated by extended family members. The town of Springerville is shown below about 1896. (Above, Becker/Harper collection; below, WMHS/Pat Christiansen.)

Illustrated above are adobes bricks being produced in 1909. Lucy Silva estimated that it took between 6,000 and 8,000 bricks to build a four-room house, and the cost was about $1,000. Pictured below is the house of Sam and Emma Saffell in Springerville. Originally made of adobes and logs, sheets of tin were attached to the outside walls in 1912, making the house look like it was made of rock from a distance. Today this house can be seen in the White Mountain Historic Park at Springerville. (Above, Apache-Sitgreaves; below, Ellis collection.)

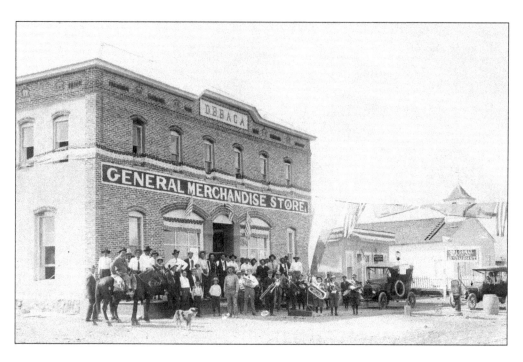

Dionicio Baca owned and operated the store above. This image shows a band in front, possibly from Magdelena, New Mexico. Below is a photograph that A. L. Westgard, national automobile road explorer, took of a Hispanic wedding in Springerville between 1910 and 1913. The procession was led by the bride and groom and three musicians, two playing violins and the other a guitar. Westgard wrote, "As we drove to one side to make room for the procession the groom halted its march, came over to our car and handed me a written invitation to attend a dance with refreshments that evening at the house of the bride's father." (Both Trish Patterson.)

In June 1881, LDS leaders from Apache and Navajo Counties met to form a cooperative store to be known as the Arizona Cooperative Mercantile Institution or ACMI. David Udall, Peter Christofferson, and Edward Noble represented St. Johns, Springerville, and Eagar respectively, and stores were set up in each of these towns. In 1913, the Springerville and Eagar stores advertised, "Make our stores your headquarters while in our villages," and the crest on the Springerville building, seen above, still contained the letters "A.C.M.I." with "Mercantile" in the black band. Shortly thereafter, ACMI was removed, and "Springerville Mercantile Company" was added. The ACMI building in Eagar was later called the Modern Store. Below is the early LDS church. (Above, ACHS/St. Johns; below, FHC/St. Johns.)

The first resident Catholic priest was Fr. Pedro Maria Badilla, who arrived in St. Johns on August 2, 1880. He named the church there San Juan Bautista. Then he established churches at Concho (San Rafael) and at Springerville (St. Peter). In 1927, the J. J. Baca Hall, a silent movie theater and dance hall, burned, and Baca donated the land for a new Catholic church. Jenano Acosta, from St. Johns, was the architect, and the Charles Herbella family donated the pews. Some of the statues inside were donated by the Joe Baca, Gregorio Baca, Harris Miller, Alexander McKay, and Ramon Almondoz families. The girls shown at left are unidentified but represent all children receiving First Communion. (Above, Trish Patterson; at left, Fidencio Baca.)

Naciancenio Gonzales, seen at right, worked at the Becker Mercantile store and was elected a member of the 22nd Territorial Legislature in 1903. He introduced bills relating to furnishing schoolbooks, recording of notary bonds and oaths, compensation for certain county offices, and relief for Aceana Tafolla, whose husband Carlos had been killed while serving as an Arizona Ranger. Nevertheless, before statehood, Arizona passed a literacy test that disenfranchised most Hispanics. As a member of the First State Legislature in 1912, Gonzales unsuccessfully attempted to reverse this requirement. In 1921, John H. Udall also introduced a bill to waive this test because, as the *Los Angeles Times* reported, "Many of these Apache county pioneers are wealthy and heavy taxpayers." Unfortunately, Udall's bill died in the Senate. Below is Naciancenio's son Senito. (At right, David Silva; below, Fidencio Baca.)

The military always needed hay for the horses at Fort Apache. Every farmer and rancher also needed hay for winter feed. Native grasses were sometimes cured, but irrigated land produced the largest yields. This hay comes from the Thompson's Ranch on the West Fork Crossing of the Black River. (WMHS.)

Although this 1937 image shows a field with shocked grain ready to be threshed near Alpine, the scene could have been much earlier or much later. Willard Skousen owned a thresher and raised grain on his grandfather James Niels Skousen's homestead. In 1982, Willard grew his last crop of oats, cut and shocked them, and showed interested schoolchildren the historic process. (Photograph by Max Hunt.)

The threshing machine above is on the Hulsey farm at Nutrioso; the machine below is probably on Crosby land and may be the same machine. James Colter threshed his first crop of barley in 1872 using sheep to trample the seed heads. The next year, he had a threshing machine shipped from Atchison, Kansas. He commented that "it cost me more to get it across the plains than the machine cost." This machine is powered by approximately 10 horses walking in a circle. Gus Becker had a steam tractor that powered a thresher. (Above, Apache-Sitgreaves; below, LaVerl Crosby.)

34

In 1909, these young people from Eagar lined up for their picture. Many of the founding families of Eagar are represented here. From left to right are Hy Wiltbank, Sadie Burk, Carrie Rencher, Bert Crosby, Joe Udall, Dell Brown, George Lytle, Lila Burgess, Jennie Greenwood, Delesa Rencher, Rinda Love, Harry Udall, Edgar Burk, Albina Greer, Hartley Greenwood, Wilmirth Hamblin, Burk Hamblin, Nell Lytle, Bailey Nelson, and Jim Greer. At left on the opposite page, also from 1909, is the main street in Eagar showing the wide, tree-lined road characteristic of Mormon villages throughout the West. (Both LaVerl Crosby.)

The first Latter-day Saints traveling through Pleasant Valley, 14 miles east of Alpine and into New Mexico, were William and Melvin Swapp, who drove cattle from Utah to Mexico in 1881. In February 1883, William Swapp, John Swapp, Elizabeth Swapp, and Lorenzo Watson brought their families to settle. Land was purchased from Alonzo Fay, but in April, Solomon Luna (at left) and his brother arrived with sheep ready to lamb in the area he had been using for years. After long, difficult discussions, the dispute was settled; Mormon settlers stayed, but the town eventually became known as Luna. Other early settlers included the families of William Reynolds, Braman Reynolds, William Laney, Willis Coplan, Samuel Adair, David Lee, and H. B. Clark. A sawmill, farming, and ranching supported the community. A 1928 photograph (below) shows early settlers in front of the school built of bricks from Stuart Russell's kiln. (At left, CSWR/New Mexico 000-021-0108; below, ACHS/St. Johns.)

Family tradition states that one of the earliest visitors to the White Mountains was William Maxwell. He traveled through southern Arizona with the Mormon Battalion the winter of 1846–1847 and, supposedly on his journey from California to Utah, traveled through Arizona, including the White Mountains. In Utah, Maxwell settled at Moccasin Springs, 18 miles southwest of Kanab. He came to Alpine in 1879. (Mesa Historical Society.)

Some of the early settlers at Alpine, originally called Bush Valley, included the Allred, Black, Burk, Hamblin, Coleman, Jepson, Judd, Lillywhite, Maxwell, McFate, Mortensen, Standifird, Skousen, Tenney, and Winsor families. Beginning in the late 1920s, residents would gather for an "Old Folks" or "Old Settlers" reunion. This image from about 1932 is in front of the two-room school/church, originally built in 1930 and on the National Register of Historic Places. (FHC/St. Johns.)

Northeastern Arizona produced many good musicians. At left is Lyman Hamblin, an early violinist; below, from left to right, are Len Jensen, Kenner Kartchner, Claude Youngblood, and Quill Stanifird, who formed an early group that played for many dances. Joe Pearce wrote that when cowboys rode through the small villages, they would say, "What brand of flour are you goin' to dance with tonight, Joe?" Thrifty Mormons reused flour sacks, and when the girls washed their underwear and hung it out to dry, passersby could read, "Pride of Denver" in big red letters; at other ranches, the underwear would say, "Pride of Colorado," "Butterfly," or "Sea Foam Fancy Flour." Pearce stated, "I tell this mostly to show the kind of life that folks [lived] on the frontier of the Arizona Territory." (At left, FHC/St. Johns; below, Nadine Trickey.)

Two

RUSTLERS, RANGERS, AND WINCHESTERS

"I am no angel and have seen most of the tough towns of the West," wrote A. F. Banta in his memoirs, "but Springerville was the worst of them all." Although Springerville's infamous outlaws may have multiplied with time, cattle rustling combined with drinking and carousing left its mark. Possibly the first group to achieve notoriety was the Cavanaugh-Snider gang from Colorado and Utah. Eight or nine members were killed near the present-day Eagar cemetery—from a quarrel over the division of gold worth about $12,000. Eagar resident Joe Pearce described this area as "the last stamping ground of the outlaw roughs and the range bad boys and the old time gamblers with quick fingers."

Cattle rustling was particularly bad in Apache County's isolated mountain valleys. Cattle thieves liked to operate along borders (United States and Mexico, Wyoming and Colorado, Arizona and New Mexico) because purloined livestock could be driven easily into the adjoining territory, thus stymieing law enforcement. Well-organized stockmen's associations brought national attention to the problem. During the 1899 National Livestock Association Convention, W. S. Seavey of Utah called for a committee of four to help Arizona's territorial governor Nathan O. Murphy find a solution. However, it was two years before Arizona took action. Burton C. Mossman claimed to have written legislation with Southern Pacific lawyer Frank Cox shortly after attending a livestock convention in Salt Lake City in January 1901. This bill established a state law enforcement agency patterned after the famed Texas Rangers to combat territorial crime and rustling in particular. The 21st Arizona Legislature easily passed the measure in March. By the end of August, Mossman had received his commission and was appointed captain of the Arizona Rangers.

The inscription on the west side of the "Madonna of the Trail" statue in Springerville reads, "A tribute to the pioneers of Arizona and the Southwest who trod this ground and braved the dangers of the Apaches and other warrior tribes." In 1938, however, 82-year-old Gus Becker lifted an eyebrow while looking at the monument and commented, "Troubles with the Indians? Hell, all our troubles came from white men."

Roy Wilhelm stated that "a thin line separated the *Law* from the *Lawless*," but "in the main we can be justly proud of our lawmen." He also published a photograph of a cowboy sitting on his horse with a rifle in his scabbard and a pistol on his hip. He wrote, "The unknown traveler—friend or enemy?" These two cowboys, George Winson (left) and David Eaton, could likewise be either. (ACHS/St. Johns.)

John Addison Hunt of Snowflake wrote, "Every outlaw carried a six-shooter—a big .45 Colt revolver—and usually a Winchester rifle, but really the only safety for a man was to be without a gun," because an unwritten Western code dictated no shooting of unarmed men. However, nearly everyone was armed, including Clyde Finch, Bert Marble, and John Norton, who are pictured here from left to right. In 1887, the Mormon bishop in Eagar encouraged men to keep their guns handy and loaded. (Iris Finch.)

The most famous sheriff of Apache County was the long-haired Commodore Perry Owens. Two other early sheriffs were Sylvester Peralta (right), from 1903 to 1904 and 1907 to 1914, and Jacob "Jake" Hamblin Jr. (below), from 1915 to 1916 and 1919 to 1920. Hamblin had to contend with bootleggers (particularly D. B. Baca and Clay Hunter) and gambling (particularly in St. Johns). From 1931 to 1932, Hamblin ran the Fort Grant Industrial School in southern Arizona and worked to make conditions more humane for the boys. One little boy, Robert Robles from Tucson, would sing hymns for Hamblin and visiting dignitaries. Perhaps Hamblin's greatest compliment came from this boy, who wished he "could live with you all my life, it is easy to do right when I am with you, and to do right makes me happy." (Both FHC/St. Johns.)

The date (December 25, 1886) and place (in front of the Brighton Saloon) may be the only points of agreement concerning the death of James Hale. He was killed either by a stray bullet or by a man who "wanted to see if a bullet would go through a Mormon." His killer has been identified variously as the Ace of Diamonds, the Jack of Diamonds, Tom Tolbert, or remnants of the Butch Cassidy Gang. (Rudy Hale.)

John Ray Hamblin called Oscar Schultz "a small time outlaw" who was shot when he came out of the Blue Lookout ranger cabin as ordered. "After all," wrote Hamblin, "he was a dangerous outlaw and they had been chasing him for several days." According to Emer Wiltbank, the men started to bury him, but remembering they needed an inquest, loaded the body on a horse and started toward Springerville. At Big Lake, they met the coroner, held the inquest, and buried Schultz. (Emer Wiltbank.)

These two young men above, Frank LeSueur (right) and Will Sherwood, were part of a posse put together by Sheriff Edward Beeler in March 1900. Beeler was in Springerville when he received word from the mail driver that five men, thought to be part of the Smith gang, had killed a beef. The posse pursued the men to St. Johns and beyond. Needing fresh horses, the posse then split into small groups. Unfortunately, LeSueur and Andrew "Gus" Gibbons were ambushed north of St. Johns (below). After killing and robbing Gibbons and LeSueur (even taking their hats), the outlaws continued on and were never captured. LeSueur's brother James was on a mission in England and received this telegram: "Released. Outlaws killed Frank. Can you sail on Anchoria, Glasgow, Friday. Platte D. Lyman." (Both ACHS/St. Johns.)

In January 1901, Ed Beeler shot and killed Monte Slaughter at Sam Saffell's saloon in Springerville. Three months later, Beeler himself was shot at this gate and managed to run as far as where Margaret Jarvis is standing. No one was arrested for the killing, and Milo Wiltbank wrote, "Who was to blame, Slaughter, Beeler / Both were shot and died / Or would you just blame the bottle / That lay there at Montie's side." (ACHS/St. Johns.)

Burton Mossman, pictured here, a poker buddy of Governor Murphy and former employee of the Aztec Land and Cattle Company, was a successful lawman. Well connected politically and socially, he was a logical choice for captain of the Arizona Rangers at its inception in 1901. Mossman hired 13 men at $55 per month for one-year enlistments. In September, Carlos Tafolla (also spelled Tafoya) of St. Johns and Duane Hamblin of Nutrioso received Ranger commissions. (*1900 National Live Stock Association Convention*.)

The first week of October 1901, the Bill Smith Gang of Blue River in northern Graham County was seen heading south from Springerville with a band of horses, presumably stolen. A posse was organized that included Rangers Hamblin (pictured at right with wife Susan Greer) and Tafolla, plus Henry Barrett, Hank Sharp, Pete Peterson, and Elijah Holgate. At Lorenzo Crosby's ranch on the Black River, three more men were added: Crosby, Arch Maxwell, and Bill Maxwell. They passed Pete Slaughter's ranch, and on October 8 arrived at a spot on the Black River that became known as the Battle Ground. Ranger Tafolla (below) and Bill Maxwell were killed, and the posse fruitlessly pursued the gang into New Mexico. Bill and Al Smith probably fled to Argentina; George Smith returned in 1909 to run cattle for his mother but was never prosecuted. (At right, FHC/ St. Johns; below, Ellis collection.)

Many posses were made up of local residents, who could be deputized at a moment's notice. Elijah Holgate participated in the Smith/Tafolla pursuit and is pictured here with other local men about 1910. From left to right they are (first row) Spencer Burk and H. Reynolds; (second row) Cleve Wiltbank, Francis Day, and Elijah Holgate. (FHC/St. Johns.)

Posse participation could simply be hazardous. Lorenzo Crosby was threatened by the Bill Smith Gang and was thus called on a mission for the LDS Church. When returning home, he was shot and killed when on the train at Kansas City, possibly by members of the gang. His widow, Mary (seen here with son Lester Lorenzo Crosby), later married John Butler and was the Mollie Butler who operated Butler's Lodge in Greer. (Wink Crigler, Little House Museum.)

Violence was not limited to outlaws, rustlers, or conflicts between people of different backgrounds. The shoot-out that Roy Wilhelm stated, "Rocked the social structure of the whole country," was in 1903 between two Latter-day Saints, old friends and substantial businessmen Prime Coleman Jr. and Henry Barrett. They argued over grazing rights in the White Mountains and settled it with their Winchesters. The shooting was witnessed by 11-year-old Jay Patterson. Both men were presumed dead. Coleman, however, recovered (originally at the home of John Sherwood, father-in-law of Barrett), and the verdict of his trial was self-defense. Below is Prime Coleman Sr. with his daughter-in-law Minnie (wife of Prime Jr.) and two grandchildren. Later Prime Jr. married Laverna Sherwood. At right, from left to right, are siblings Prime Jr. (age 73), Etta Pomeroy (83), and Evans (69) at Safford. (At right, AHS/Tucson 11,215; below, FHC/St. Johns.)

In 1903, Capt. Thomas Rynning and Gov. Alexander Brodie were looking to appoint a Ranger from Navajo or Apache County. Joe Pearce was "hankering after a change" and "couldn't get gun matter out of my *cabeza*." Rynning wanted men who were single, proficient in Spanish, knowledgeable about cattle, and able to provide themselves with a horse, saddle, complete pack outfit, Colt .45 six-shooter, and a Carbine .30–.40. Pearce already had a reputation for law enforcement acumen following three years working for the Forest Service. He joined at Douglas; his Ranger time was never in Apache or Navajo Counties. Later he married Minnie Lund (seen here) from Nutrioso, and the couple celebrated their golden wedding anniversary on November 7, 1956. A friend, Ralph Penrod, fiddled at both their wedding and golden wedding parties. (Neal Pearce.)

The Arizona Rangers were organized to rid the territory of "bad men, undesirable citizens, cattle rustlers, gamblers, and motley border renegades," wrote Charlie Niehuis in 1937. As a law enforcement organization operating outside the legal system, historians give the Rangers a mixed review. Niehuis stated they "saw action in the field and dissention among themselves, their political affiliates and the general public." After eight years they were disbanded with "private charges hurled at the organization." However, in the 1940s and 1950s, their accomplishments were generally celebrated. They were invited to ride in Tucson's La Fiesta de los Vaqueros, where Oliver Parmer, O. C. Wilson, Jim Bailey, C. A. Epperson, Rye Miles, Joe Pearce, and Charles McGarr are pictured from left to right in February 1940. About 1956, they met with Gov. Ernest McFarland. Pictured below at this meeting, from left to right, are Pearce, Rube Neill, McFarland, Parmer, and John Redmond. (Above, AHS/Tucson 7,756; below, AHS/Tucson 43,915.)

From 1957–1959, some 78 episodes of the television program *26 Men* were broadcast. Joe Pearce, Chapo Beatty, and John Redmond acted as advisors, and Joe received a gold watch, chain, and cigarette lighter as a memento. One Ranger researcher, however, recently stated, "The episodes were all supposed to be based on true incidents—most I can't find any records of." Shot on location in Arizona in March 1958, producer Russell Hayden suddenly had complaints about the clutter of stagecoaches, armed riders, and movie equipment. He found his permit was for the Salt River Indian Reservation while he was filming on the Fort McDowell Reservation. From left to right above are Rangers Chapo Beatty, Joe Pearce, Oliver Parmer, and Jack Redmond on the movie set. Below, from left to right, are (first row) Redmond, Beatty, Pearce, and Parmer; (second row) actors, Tris Coffin, who played Captain Rynning, and Kelo Henderson, the fictitious Ranger Clint Travis. (Above, AHS/Tucson 43,916; below, AHS/Tucson 43,917.)

In 1957, former Arizona Rangers and other interested parties created a civilian law enforcement auxiliary also named the Arizona Rangers. Ranger companies throughout the state donate countless hours assisting federal, state, and local law enforcement organizations with public safety. The Arizona Rangers also support local youth groups. Despite volunteer status, prospective recruits undertake training, qualify with weapons, and take an oath prior to admittance. In September 2008, the Rangers came to Apache County to honor Duane Hamblin and Joe Pearce (above). No members of Hamblin's family still lived in Apache County, but many of the children and grandchildren of Joe and Minnie Pearce attended the ceremony (below). (Both Neal Pearce.)

Arizona Rangers posing for this photograph at Morenci following the strike of 1903 are, from left to right, Capt. Thomas Rynning, John Foster, Jack Campbell, W. D. Allison, T. S. Barfoot, O. C. Wilson, F. S. Wheeler, J. O. Mullen, Oscar Felton, Billy Sparks, R. M. Anderson, W. S. Peterson, J. H. Bassett, Tip Stanford, William "Tex" Fergusson, Sam Henshaw, Charles Rie, Arthur Hopkins, James D. Bailey, W. W. Webb, Henry Gray, C. L. Beatty, D. E. Wareford, J. T. Holmes, and A. R. McDonald (Jeff Kidder was absent). In 1962, Winchester published part of this photograph with the caption, "19 Texas Rangers; only 18 Winchesters. Why?" (Charles Rie had a Krag.) Ranger Joe Pearce later stated, "Even though most of us carried Winchesters, we figured the best rifle on the market in those days was the Spanish Mauser. . . . We regarded it as even better than the Cragg [sic]-Jorgenson." The Krag (shown opposite page, bottom, with a Winchester above it) was a bolt-action rifle, and Winchester used a lever action. Both shot the same ammunition, which could always be found at army posts. (Above, AHS/Tucson 14,364; opposite page, photograph by David Ellis.)

This photograph was also taken at Morenci, and many Arizonans recognized Winchester's error (Texas versus Arizona Rangers). Roscoe Willson featured the story in his September 2, 1962, *Arizona Republic* column. Winchester immediately began apologizing. In September 1963, Winchester sent their director of advertising to Arizona stating, "And [he] will do anything he's told, like cleaning every last Winchester rifle in the state." They provided reprint sepia posters to local Winchester-Western dealers "with that goldarn printing removed. So you can pick one up. And hang it. In your home." They issued a formal apology, "We offer our sincere apologies to the people of Arizona, to the Arizona Rangers, and especially to those who have called our attention to this embarrassing mistake." Then they presented Gov. Paul Fannin with a Winchester model 94 to be known as the "Arizona Apology Gun," which was displayed at Steinfeld's 7th Annual Gun Show in Tucson in August 1964. Finally, company officials sponsored a "Winchester Apology Dinner" at the Mountain Shadows Resort in Paradise Valley and honored Minnie Pearce, widow of Ranger Joe Pearce. (AHS/Tucson 45,753.)

Three

THE FOREST RESERVES

"Only the mountain has lived long enough to listen objectively to the howl of a wolf," wrote Aldo Leopold, the most influential wildlife ecologist of the early 20th century. Leopold lived in the White Mountains only two short years. In *A Sand County Almanac*, he wrote, "Despite several opportunities to do so, I have never returned to the White Mountains. I prefer not to see what tourists, roads, sawmills, and logging railroads have done for it, or to it. I hear young people, not yet born when I first rode out 'on top,' exclaim about it as a wonderful place. To this, with an unspoken mental reservation, I agree."

Aldo Leopold was born in Iowa in 1887 and joined the U.S. Forest Service in 1909. His description of the White Mountains, and Escudilla in particular, come from this last-of-the-pioneers era. The area then went through a period of fire suppression, predator removal, and extensive logging before some of Leopold's ecological principles were applied. He later expressed understanding for the role predators play in keeping a deer population healthy when he wrote, "In those days we had never heard of passing up a chance to kill a wolf. . . . When our rifles were empty, the old wolf was down, and a pup was dragging a leg into impassable slide-rocks." As the Forest Service men watched the "fierce green fire dying in her eyes," Leopold recognized that "neither the wolf nor the mountain" agreed that "fewer wolves meant more deer [and] that no wolves would mean hunters' paradise."

Not long ago, wolves were reintroduced to the White Mountains with mixed results and strong feelings. Ranchers deplore depredations by the wolf, while conservationists insist that species preservation should be paramount. Leopold wrote, "The cowman who cleans his range of wolves does not realize that he is taking over the wolf's job of trimming the herd to fit the range. He has not learned to think like a mountain. Hence we have dustbowls, and rivers washing the future into the sea." Perhaps one day, everyone will "think like a mountain."

Arizona residents have always come to the White Mountains to enjoy cool summer days in the pines. Pictured above are young people from St. Johns enjoying a picnic about 1900. From left to right they are (first row) Pearl Peterson, Sophia Gibbons, Lydia Platt, Edith Waite, Alice Berry, Sylvia Peterson, and Hattie Platt; (second row) Ben Gibbons, Will Gibbons, Will Stratton, Martin Jensen, and B. Y. Peterson. Note that each young man has brought his six-shooter, and all but Will Gibbons have brought a rifle to the picnic. Below is another group, probably from St. Johns, that has come to the White Mountains for a Fourth of July celebration. (Both ACHS/St. Johns.)

Elliot Barker described early Forest Service Rangers as "ranch-and-cowboy type of men." Pictured at right is Leo Eagar at the Gentry Ranger Station in typical Ranger uniform: Levi Strauss or khaki pants, work shirt, blue denim jacket, and Stetson with chaps and/or gloves added in brushy country. Aldo Leopold described the White Mountains as "the exclusive domain of the mounted man." Everyone traveled by horseback. In the railroad towns of Holbrook and Winslow, a person could travel by "shoe leather, burro, cowhorse, buckboard, freight wagon, caboose, or Pullman," but on the Mogollon Rim and before the advent of the automobile, "the horseman ruled the world." Unidentified Forest Service men and their mounts are seen below at John Kerr's cabin in the Tularosa District, New Mexico. (At right, Wanda Turley Smith; below, Apache-Sitgreaves.)

A. O. Waha, one of the first technically trained foresters, came to New Mexico in 1905. In 1908, he was working at Springerville (above 1912, below 1926) and needed to visit the headquarters of the Sitgreaves National Forest at Show Low. He rented a horse and thought he "would have no difficulty in reaching Show Low by dark." But after 13 hours of wind, snow, and muddy roads, he decided to camp. With no bedroll and a horse that wanted to go back to Springerville, he had a miserable night and "daylight came none too soon to suit me." After a breakfast of the previous night's tongue sandwich, he soon found himself in Show Low. "I had been on the hill above Show Low when I was out reconnoitering, and could have seen the town if there had been any lights in any of the houses," he wrote. "The Mormons had the habit of going to bed early." (Both Apache-Sitgreaves.)

Benton Rogers (above right) was an itinerant cowboy when John Guthrie and Waha (above left) first met him in 1909. Guthrie and Waha found themselves without camping equipment one evening in Hog Canyon. They asked to share Rogers's tent. Later Rogers remembered, "I told them O.K., that I could stand it if they could. I had a blanket on back of the saddle. I told 'em I'd give 'a part of my bed, and we'd make it all right.' " The next morning they asked Rogers what he thought about the Forest Service. "Never heard of it," he said, and they encouraged him to apply as a fireguard. Rogers worked 30 years on the Apache National Forest. From left to right (below) are four Rangers and three candidates in 1909: J. H. Sizer, unidentified, Joe Pearce, unidentified, Rogers, unidentified, and J. L. Prichard. (Above, AHS/Tucson 17,153; below, Apache-Sitgreaves.)

Aldo Leopold, pictured above, was 22 years old when he came to the Apache National Forest in 1909. He was immediately assigned to head a timber reconnaissance party, which surveyed the forest to find out how much timber could be harvested. Leopold was green and struggled through the first year. His second year was much better. The foresters had both double and single tents, cots to sleep on, and a wagon to move camp every few days. The cook's biscuits, however, were heavy, and the men named their camp "Camp Indigestion." The picture below, taken on July 26, 1910, shows the reconnaissance party with Aldo Leopold and John D. Guthrie on the far right. (Both Apache-Sitgreaves.)

A. E. Douglass at the University of Arizona first proposed dendrochronology (tree-ring dating) in the 1920s. The technique works best in arid or semiarid climates and uses either cross sections or core samples. It is used to date timbers in buildings and art objects, as well as to understand drought cycles. Ray Kingston is pictured at right drilling a core sample on the Roosevelt Tree that has "T. Roosevelt 1904" carved into the trunk. About 2000, U.S. Forest Service officials tried using tree-ring dating to authenticate the name and date. The carvings are so high that the author was probably standing on a wagon, and most Theodore Roosevelt historians do not believe that he came to Arizona in 1904. Unfortunately, dating was unsuccessful due to degradation of the wood. (Both Apache-Sitgreaves.)

For transporting logs to a mill, Forest Service supervisor Edward Miller remembered that big wheels (above) were used "most of the time in the summer [and] in winter, on snow, they used what they called drays, which were big sleds." Many men throughout the White Mountains made their living as contract loggers. Miller also stated that some of the Mormons brought in four- or eight-wheel wagons. Below, Nahum Marble (left) and John Rush Norton of Eagar are hauling logs with a team and an eight-wheel wagon. (Above, Apache-Sitgreaves; below, Iris Finch.)

The man in the photograph at right (here in New Mexico) illustrates the size of logs coming out of old-growth forests. Forest Service Rangers worked as scalers, pictured below, measuring diameter to estimate the board feet of lumber from the tree. Frederick Winn's "Forest Service Fables" included a little story: "It is related of a New Mexico ranger that one day as he was passing a ranch house he was called in by the rancher. Upon entering he was asked to measure the rancher's wife for a corset. The ranger being familiar with the manner of taking the diameters of trees took the measurement but failed to enter the job in his diary at the end of the day. His explanation was that he was uncertain whether to charge it to Improvement (Maintenance) or Unclassified." (At right, Thomason/Ellis collection; below, Apache-Sitgreaves.)

The Whiting brothers owned stores, service stations, farms, cattle ranches, motels, truck lines, contracting firms, and lumber mills in four states and employed many of their friends and neighbors. Pictured above, from left to right, they are Edwin "E. I.," Ralph, Ernest, and Arthur. About 1905, E. I. had $6,000 from two bumper crops of barley that he sold to the army at Fort Apache. With this he bought 100 head of cattle, a small store, and a small sawmill. With hard work and the practice of collecting overdue accounts in labor, the empire grew. At left, Beulah Whiting, daughter of Ernest, is standing on a stack of lumber ready for sale. (Above, ACHS/St. Johns; at left, Wanda Turley Smith.)

The Springerville-Eagar area has had many other sawmills, large and small. About 1890, Bill Cross worked for Bob Tyler at Alpine in a "pony saw mill." Ellis "Ett" Wiltbank operated the sawmill pictured here at Greer, 16 miles southwest of Eagar. Later there were mills on Apache lands. (ACHS/St. Johns.)

Francis Day Sr. operated this shingle mill in 1910. He also had sawmills and gristmills and was a logging contractor. He burned lime, made bricks, and quarried rocks. Later, with his sons Francis Jr. and Marlow, he had Apache County's largest sand, rock, and cement company. (Apache-Sitgreaves.)

Tom Pollock of Flagstaff built the original sawmill at Cluff Cienega in 1917 and named the town Cooley. The mill, however, closed after World War I. In 1924, M. W. Cady and James G. McNary purchased the mill and leases from the Apache Tribe and went to New York to secure $2 million for improvements. Eventually the lumber company became Southwest Lumber, and the town became McNary. James McNary was president of the company from 1924 to 1950. Mona Campbell described the town in 1960 as "picturesque," and "a company town completely dependent for its existence upon a large sawmill and its logging operations." In 1947, a 68-mile railroad spur was added, and Maverick Camp was born. The company store at Maverick is shown below. (Above, Apache-Sitgreaves; below, Keith Eagar.)

Both McNary and Maverick were segregated. Although Mona Campbell credited McNary with "peaceful racial relations," the homes were not all equal. This photograph of Maverick shows Hispanic houses in the foreground and white houses across the meadow. Out of view in the photograph are black homes on the left and Apache houses on the right. Maverick was on Apache land, but the tribe received little compensation for timber cut. (Keith Eagar.)

Maverick often reported the coldest temperatures in the United States (with Yuma often reporting the hottest). Winter snow was deep as seen in this dramatic photograph of the Apache Railway, which Fairbanks-Morse used to advertise their diesel-electric engine. The advertisement began "Elevation: 9,000 feet [sic], Satisfaction: 100 percent" and noted "no noticeable loss of power" on "18 miles of 2.5 percent ruling grade" with loads "as high as 500 tons." (Ellis collection.)

The meadows of the White Mountains were used to pasture large herds of sheep each summer, many of which were owned by Hispanic families. Juan Candelaria from Concho was a particularly important sheep owner. Above is an unidentified young woman, probably at Concho, with orphaned or abandoned lambs. At left, sheep are crossing the Verde River Bridge as they are being driven from winter pastures in the Salt River Valley to summering areas in the White Mountains. (Above, Thomason/Ellis collection; at left, Library of Congress.)

Wool and mutton were important exports from the White Mountains. An unidentified Hispanic man (right) and a drawing of a sheep herd (below) documented this piece of history. Forest Rangers sometimes settled disputes between sheep men and cattlemen. Joe Pearce told of being appointed judge and jury at Vernon in a dispute between Bailey Leverton and the Morris brothers. Pearce concluded that the Morris brothers should pay the court costs of $10, pay $25 for damage to Leverton's corn patch, and serve dinner of coffee and mutton to the crowd. The judgment was satisfactory to both parties, and soon, to Pearce's amazement, everyone was "drinking coffee out of the same pot and eating Morris mutton, and the Levertons were out there with the rest *eating mutton*." (At right, Thomason/Ellis collection; below, *The Image of Arizona*.)

Forest Service employee Jesse Nelson wrote, "They had some sheep and cattle war-type incidents [in the White Mountains], but they never had the intense sheep and cattle wars in New Mexico and Arizona that they did in Montana and Wyoming and a part of Western Colorado where the sheep moved in . . . on an established industry. But down here, sheep were in New Mexico long before cattle." Shown at left is the remnant of a sheep dip, where the animals were run through a pesticide mixture to eliminate harmful insects. Below are cattle at Becker Lake, a holding area used for many years as cattle were waiting to be trucked to market. (At left, Emer Wiltbank; below, LaVerl Crosby.)

It is always difficult to understand the carrying capacity of land subject to intermittent drought, a problem that caused friction between the Forest Service and cattlemen with Forest Service grazing permits. The spring condition of cattle from overstocked ranges in the Apache Forest during the drought year of 1928 is shown above. Below, Alvin Lee Wilhelm of Vernon is roping cattle in better condition. He called his ranch the Tapadero Dude Ranch. Fred Winn worked at easing tensions between the Forest Service and cattlemen, and on the occasion of his retirement he was given a cowhide with the message, "To Fred Winn, who has paved the way for harmony between the stockmen and the Forest Service. We the undersigned members of the Chiricahua Cattle Growers Assn. want to extend our best wishes for happiness and luck to Fred Winn, 'A hell of a good man.' " (Above, Apache-Sitgreaves; below, Kathy Hausman.)

Two women who raised families by themselves were Ellen Camp Greer and Hannah Wilhelm (pictured here). When Hannah's husband, Bateman Haight Wilhelm, wanted advice from LDS Church leaders concerning polygamy, he was encouraged to take his wife Grace to Mexico and Joseph F. Smith thought "Sister Lydia Hannah had better remain on her homestead and perfect the title to the same." To "prove up" on a homestead, a person had to make improvements and live on the property for five years; Hannah Wilhelm received a patent for land at Concho and later also at Vernon. (Mabel Wilhelm.)

The Greer family came to Arizona from Texas in 1877 and was handy with their guns. Some thought these Mormon boys should go on missions. Charles Riggs of Concho replied, "Missions, missions, go on missions! Do you [know] what might happen to us if they went on missions? Who would we have to fight for us?" Ellen Camp Greer fed every desperado who was, she thought, just a misguided boy away from home. Shown here are two of her grandsons, Nathaniel Greer (left) and Thomas Greer (right) with their brides, sisters Edith and Nellie Thomas, respectively. (Both ACHS/St. Johns.)

Roy Wilhelm described Vernon as "a harsh and unyielding county" but "a wonderful place to raise kids—at least that is what the kids thought. No matter how poor, every kid had a horse and every one was a cowboy." Members of the Casimiro Padilla family were the first to settle at the mouth of Mineral Canyon. By 1910, a post office was established and named Vernon. Homesteaders and displaced Mormons from Mexico also settled at Vernon. At right is Zemira George Wilhelm (son of Bateman and Hannah) with his bride, Naomi Freeman. Shown in the 1945 photograph below is Alvin Lee Wilhelm (grandson of Bateman and Hannah) with his wife, Effie Lewis. (At right, Mabel Wilhelm; below, FHC/St. Johns.)

Hunting, particularly for deer, gradually changed from subsistence hunting to recreational hunting. Brothers Melvin (left) and Wyatt Crosby are pictured on Escudilla Mountain with their rifles in 1937. The photographer, Max Hunt, wrote, "Resolved some fun—no game." (Ellis collection.)

Guided hunting, however, remained popular, as illustrated in this photograph of a hunter's cabin in the White Mountains/ Blue Range. For example, the *Holbrook News* reported on September 30, 1921, that a party from California was hunting in the White Mountains with "guns of all sizes, shapes, and calibre [*sic*]." N. A. Brimhall guided the seven men on a 15-day hunting trip. Hopefully they were as successful as the five men in this photograph. (Fidencio Baca.)

Some say Benjamin Lilly (above) was the greatest hunter the United States ever produced. Former hunting companion of Theodore Roosevelt, Lilly felt he was appointed by God to rid infested areas of varmints, meaning bears and mountain lions. He was employed by both the Biological Survey and private ranchers in 1912 to work in the Blue River region. Lilly mythology includes wrestling bears hand to hand and never hunting on Sunday (unless he lost track of days). It is believed that he killed the last grizzly in Arizona. Another early bounty hunter from the White Mountains was Clay Hunter, who is believed to have killed the last Mexican gray wolf (below). (Above, Silver City Museum 759; below, Arizona Game and Fish Department, photograph by George Andrejko.)

Fishing is usually less controversial than hunting, although stocking with non-native fish, impoundments along waterways, and erosion leaving topsoil in streams can cause problems for species like the Apache trout. Big Lake regularly froze in the winter, killing all the fish, until its depth was increased. A June 1963 issue of *Arizona Wildlife and Travelogue* advertised 23 trout lakes and 680 miles of trout streams in the White Mountains. The Wiltbanks often used horses, packing guests into remote areas for fishing, including Sam Levitz from Tucson, who is pictured above (right) about 1945. The joy of fishing, however, is best illustrated by three-year-old Derick Turner, seen below, at Sheep Crossing in the 1980s. (Above, Emer Wiltbank; below, DaLane Turner.)

Pet deer, like the one pictured here, were common in early days. Nellie Fuentes of Luna used one to watch over her baby on the porch. Less common pets were the two eagles Gus Becker sent to the El Paso Zoo. The eagles had originally belonged to his son Julius, and when Julius married, Gus commented in a newspaper article that the birds were sent "where boys and girls and grown-ups, too, might enjoy them." (Thomason/Ellis collection.)

One of Arizona's most scenic and highest-elevated hikes is to the summit of Mount Baldy (Baldy Peak), Arizona's third-highest mountain. This basalt flow is about 3 miles up the trail from the East Baldy trailhead on Route 273. (Photograph by Eric Krueger.)

An important duty for early Forest Rangers was spotting and fighting fires. Early towers were simply tall trees. Kenner Kartchner helped construct a 45-foot pole tower at Deer Spring Lookout in 1913 and wrote, "My role that first summer was a combination lookout, smoke chaser, and telephone lineman— always by horseback, seven days a week." He continued, "Such limited manpower and transportation for controlling forest fires . . . would be totally inadequate today . . . however, the stands were open as a result of natural and Indian burning of ground cover [and] fires that started seldom got off the ground." At left, Mr. (tentatively identified as Guy) Rencher is locating a fire by triangulation (note the pistol in his belt). Below is the more modern Dutch Joe lookout tower in 1948. (Both Apache-Sitgreaves.)

The Forest Service was willing to give private cabins in remote areas telephone service if the ranchers who lived in them were willing to help fight fires. Some cabins had telephones and some did not. Early lines were often strung on living trees (at right, in the Blue Range in 1913). One of the worst fires was in 1951 on Escudilla Mountain. The year was dry, and a careless smoker began a fire that consumed trees on 19,500 acres of Forest Service land and another 240 acres in private ownership. The fire burned out of control for eight days and then was brought under control by a freak snowstorm on July 2. Forest Service employees (below) are shown replanting trees after this fire. (Both Apache-Sitgreaves.)

This picnic at the fish hatchery grounds involved visitors from Phoenix, including Gov. George W. P. Hunt. (ACHS/St. Johns.)

Many early pioneers, particularly those with grazing permits or homes on Forest Service land or inholdings, shared personal photographs with the Forest Service. The Wiltbank home, located on the west side of the Little Colorado River at Greer, is the setting for this photograph taken at the time of the wedding of W. S. Gibbons and Ida Wiltbank in 1901. Pictured here from left to right are John Hall, Florence Wiltbank, Alice Butler, Ann Butler, Mae Hale, Effie Butler, Ashley Hall, and Laura Burgess. (Apache-Sitgreaves.)

During the Great Depression, one of President Roosevelt's most successful programs was the Civilian Conservation Corps (CCC). Pictured above is an unidentified CCC camp in the White Mountains. White Mountain camps included F-04-A (near Alpine and Jackson Springs), Blue (mouth of Johnson Canyon), Buffalo Crossing (east fork of the Black River), Greer, and Three Forks (east of Big Lake). Men in these camps were usually not from the area. They built lookout towers, improved campgrounds and roads, fought fires, installed telephone lines, exterminated prairie dogs, and built dams for erosion control. The Greer camp made a small boat to help in surveying and then allowed local children to use it. Local men went to other camps: James Norton, Wilford Bigelow, and Marion Hamblin worked at Los Burros; Rudolfo Peña Jr., pictured below, went to Carson. (Above, Apache-Sitgreaves; below, Fidencio Baca.)

The number of visitor days in the national forests of the Southwest is now counted in the millions instead of thousands. In the 1930s, Landis "Pink" Arnold was chosen to head CCC construction of recreational facilities because, as Zane Smith recalled, Arnold "had scrounged around and managed to build out in the [Sandia Mountains in New Mexico] a few old tables out of scrap lumber and give some attention to the recreationists out of Albuquerque." CCC men constructed facilities for both camping and picnicking. Shown above is an early summer camp in the Baldy Primitive Area; below is a 1948 camp at Big Lake. (Both Apache-Sitgreaves.)

Four

GUS BECKER'S HIGHWAY

Anthon L. Westgard drove an automobile into Springerville in November 1910. He wrote, "On my first trip into the Apache country I had been assured that if I could only reach Springerville, gasoline would undoubtedly be found at that settlement," but the only gasoline available was in the store lamps. Gus Becker thought Westgard could get more at Fort Apache, so the Pathfinder and his crew proceeded—through a blizzard. At Fort Apache, they again found no gasoline, but the three officers were delighted to have a fourth hand for whist. As the men played through the night, Westgard was contemplating a two-week stay while freighters traveled to Holbrook for the precious fluid. Then the captain's "boy" came in to get uniforms to clean. Suddenly Westgard had an idea. Upon quizzing the boy and then the quartermaster, four or five gallons of cleaning fluid were found. Westgard concluded, "The next morning this very fluid made the engine frisky as a colt and the contents of the quartermaster's 'cleaning fluid' container enabled me to reach Globe, 60 miles distant."

In 1910, automobiles were fast becoming a national craze. Men like Henry Ford and Ransom Olds began marketing affordable machines for working class families, while songs such as "In My Merry Oldsmobile" became popular. With improved roads, tourism and recreation became important industries in the West. Developers and local residents alike began to capitalize on business as touring and automobile clubs were organized. As early as 1896, Arizona began promoting itself with publications such as *Border Magazine* and *Progressive Arizona*. By the 1930s, some estimated that tourism would bring in $75 million, while automobile taxes, licenses, and penalties would generate $3,236,896.35.

As part of this trend, Arizona organized its own branch of the American Automobile Association (AAA) with Gus Becker as an advisory board member. Their official publication, *The Arizona Magazine*, promoted both tourism and safe driving, and it frequently featured the White Mountains as a vacation destination.

In 1929, the *Miami Silver Belt* called 73-year-old Gus Becker (left) the "Father of Good Roads in Arizona." Becker was described as having smiling blue eyes, shining snow-white hair, and "movements [that] are as swift and decisive as those of men half a century younger." The editor continued, "There is nothing like a clean hobby to keep a man young. Gus Becker has three. They are: Good Roads for Arizona; the Development of the Natural Resources of Northern Arizona; and a third, a consuming desire that all the world, and Arizonans particularly, will come to know and enjoy the wonderful White Mountains as he does." Becker helped publish the *Arizona Good Roads Association Illustrated Road Maps and Tour Book* in 1913 (below). From Springerville to Cooley's Ranch was described as "Rough Road, Rocky Grades, Delightful Scenery." (At left, Margie Harper; below, Ellis collection.)

In 1910, Becker ordered an E-M-F (Everitt-Metzger-Flanders) automobile delivered to Magdalena, New Mexico (along with a driving instructor). This became the first locally owned car and, much to Becker's chagrin, had a narrower wheelbase than the commonly used horse-drawn wagons. After driving with one wheel in the rut and the other on the mid-road hump, Becker installed a wider axle. (Trish Patterson.)

Gustav Becker built a garage in Springerville and began selling Red Crown gasoline. He also sold Fords as early as 1914. The Model Ts were shipped to Holbrook and then driven to Springerville, a task sometimes performed by his nine-year-old grandson Gus. In 1988, this was thought to be the third-oldest Ford dealership west of the Mississippi. (Fidencio Baca.)

In 1910, the National Highway Association wanted a transcontinental automobile route mapped, so in October and November, Anthon L. Westgard and Ray McNamara traveled in a Premier from New York to Los Angeles, which took 49 days. Westgard's automobile and mapping trips, beginning in 1904, led him to be called "the Pathfinder." In spring 1911, he again passed through the White Mountains, this time in a 5-ton, Swiss-made Saurer truck. He found "bottomless mud" requiring eight and a half hours to travel two and a half miles. In November 1911, he led a transcontinental tour with eight paying customers ($875 per person, in today's dollars $19,976), six professional drivers, and a writer/photographer for *Sunset*. The caravan used Garford cars and a Garford truck labeled "The Raymond-Whitcomb Trail to Sunset" (above at Yuma). The photograph below may be one of these cars "stuck in an Arizona bog" before arriving at Cooley's Ranch. (Above, National Archives 30-N-7089; below, Apache-Sitgreaves.)

Because A. L. Westgard found snow in the White Mountains in November 1910 and again in spring 1911, he wrote in his *Tales of a Pathfinder*, "The high plateaus of Northern New Mexico and Arizona are frequently visited by an early autumn snowstorm, causing much arduous work for those motorists who happen to be afield at the time." This April 1925 photograph was taken near the Lincoln Ranger Station. (Apache-Sitgreaves.)

Barney Oldfield, pictured at the wheel of a Stutz with his signature cigar, signed Becker's tourist register. He raced bicycles, motorcycles, and cars and commented, "There is exhilaration in driving fast that I cannot resist: it is like intoxication." In November 1914, Oldfield was greeted by 5,000 Arizona State Fair attendees when he won a Los Angeles to Phoenix off-road race, earning the title "Master Driver of the World." (Thomason/Ellis collection.)

Eddie Rickenbacker is remembered as a World War I ace fighter pilot, but he also repaired and raced cars. He used his expertise and fame to build and market the Rickenbacker Six. Beginning in 1922, Rickenbacker promoted his car, often with long-distance races and records set by Erwin George "Cannon Ball" Baker, pictured above near Springerville about 1925. Years later, Baker fondly remembered his association with Gus Becker. Baker was concerned about snow in the high-elevation meadows between Springerville and McNary. Becker promised to use 30 teams of horses if necessary, pictured below, to clear the trail if Baker would come and put Springerville on the map. After seeing the cleared trail, Baker asked, "How much do I owe you?" "Not a cent," said Becker. "I'll do it again anytime you'll come to Springerville." (Both AHS/Tucson.)

Julius W. Becker wrote that Holbrook townspeople were not road-minded because they had the railroad, but Springerville merchants lobbied hard for a route connecting Springerville to Phoenix. From 1909 to 1927, Arizona roads were significantly improved with money from the 1916 Federal Aid Road Act. Max Hunt remembered construction on Highway 66 about 1925 when a berm was built using horses and Fresno or slip scrapers. The dirt from the borrow ditch on either side was piled up, leveled off, and topped with gravel. While working on the Ocean to Ocean Highway, seen above, the men devised a laborsaving way to load the wagons with roadbed material. By 1920, more men were employed on road construction than in all other state agencies. They became the main market for explosives as they tunneled through rock like that pictured below on Mule Creek Road in 1948. (Both Apache-Sitgreaves.)

As roads began to improve, tourists needed accommodations. Free campgrounds were often just outside town. Note that Becker's sign next to his garage displays the AAA symbol. In 1918, the first Ocean to Ocean Convention was held in Springerville, complete with cowboys from Eagar, Springerville, Alpine, Greer, and Nutrioso to entertain the guests. Roy Hall even rode "the wildest horse in the country" with a broken leg. (WMHS/Pat Christiansen.)

Not only did Gus Becker support better highways, but by 1928, his son Julius (pictured) was vice president of the National Old Trails Road Association. At the time, Harry S. Truman was president of the national association located in Independence, Missouri. This began a long association between the Becker family and Truman. Other men who served as vice presidents were Tobias Younis of Concho and Jay Patterson of St. Johns. (AHS/Tucson, Becker collection.)

In 1913, the Arizona Good Roads Association book advertised two hotels in Springerville, "Hotels Saffell and Reagan furnish pleasant accommodations for the traveler. Excellent meals of good things grown in the immediate vicinity. Hot and Cold Water Baths." Pictured above (left) are two guests at the Hotel Reagan in town in September 1919 for Bertrand's show *The Tempest*. A Hispanic maid (right) also poses at the same spot in front of the hotel. Below is the Saffell Hotel, which, after saloon keeper Sam Saffell's death during a shooting in St. Johns in 1913, was run by his widow, Emma, for many years. Irene and Clem Saffell stand at the left gatepost. (Above, Ellis collection; below, Trish Patterson.)

In 1928, the Daughters of the American Revolution (DAR) and the National Old Trails Association dedicated 12 identical statues from Bethesda, Maryland, to Upland, California, honoring "the Pioneer Mothers of the Covered Wagon Days." Arlene B. Nichols Moss, pictured at left (left), spearheaded the effort and selected St. Louis sculptor August Leimbach (on ladder). Each *Madonna of the Trail* sculpture is made of warm pink, poured algonite stone; the entire monument is 18 feet high. Leimbach described his vision, "The pioneer mother with her children was waiting for the father at their blockhouse in the wild West, for the father did not come home as he had promised. She, believing him to be in danger, put her little child in a blanket, grasped the gun and with the boy ran out in the field to look for the father." (Both Trish Patterson.)

Eliza Catherine Rudd, at age 96, was given the honor of unveiling the *Madonna of the Trail* at Springerville, but the veil would not come off—two boys had to climb up and help. The inscriptions on each statue reflect local history. The original statement for Springerville's Madonna mentioned Mormon pioneers, but the DAR let Julius Becker know that they "would under no circumstances recognize the Mormons." So the two inscriptions read, "Coronado passed here in 1540. He came to seek gold but found fame," and "A tribute to the pioneers of Arizona and the Southwest who trod this ground and braved the dangers of the Apaches and other warrior tribes." Many visiting dignitaries came for the dedication. At right, Gus Becker (right) is photographed with Wallace Altaha, an important Apache cattleman who was often identified by his tag number, R-14. (Above, FHC/St. Johns; at right, Ellis collection.)

Gov. George W. P. Hunt was a Democrat who loved his constituency. Many Mormons supported Hunt in his numerous elections. Hunt, seen above, mounted a burro in the parade for the *Madonna of the Trail* celebration to represent himself as he rode into Globe in October 1881. He also was photographed, at left, with C. R. Price (left), another official visitor from Phoenix. As Hunt spoke at the dedication, he said nothing had given him "as much genuine pleasure" as the dedication of this monument. He spoke of Coronado, the waves of Spanish American immigrants, the California Argonauts of 1849, the cattle barons from Texas, and the "pioneer Mormon women [who] faced incessant fatigue and constant danger . . . [so] they might worship their God according to the dictates of their own conscience." (Above, FHC/St. Johns; at left, ACHS/St. Johns.)

The *Madonna of the Trail* has been dedicated three times: first, on September 29, 1928, when it was installed; second, when it was moved across the street in 1987; and third, in 1998 for its 70th anniversary, seen above. Originally the Madonna stood in front of the post office. Then it was moved when the highway was widened, and it was moved again in 1987 across the street to its present location. This difficult move is illustrated at right. (Both Fidencio Baca.)

In May 1901, John Guthrie was asked to locate a suitable road from Springerville south to Clifton. His assessment was that it would be possible but expensive. To illustrate, Gus Becker wrote on a faded photograph of a couple with a horse and buggy, "Springerville to Clifton, 183 river crossings." Early travel in this area was so difficult that it was easier for people in Clifton to use the railroad and go to El Paso, Texas, for merchandise and doctor visits. Because money came from the federal government, and with the interruption of World War I, the Coronado Trail was not completed until 1926. It was dedicated with great fanfare in June (above and below). Gov. George W. P. Hunt attended, and Apaches came to the festivities to dance for the visitors. (Above, AHS/Tucson 17,078; below, Apache-Sitgreaves.)

The Coronado Trail may be the least traveled federal highway, in part because of the many switchbacks and hairpin turns. It commemorates Francisco Vasquez de Coronado's 1540 explorations of Arizona, although it probably does not follow his route. It also may be the only highway renumbered because of a Bible passage. With Revelation 13:18 identifying 666 as the "number of the beast," Highway 666 was changed to Highway 191. The men above are opening the road during the winter of 1936–1937. Pictured below is the Arizona Livestock Association being served dinner in 1938. (Both Apache-Sitgreaves.)

Many ranchers supplemented their income with guests. Jess L. Burk of Alpine listed himself as a farmer in 1930, but he was a legendary bear and mountain lion hunter. He built the Beaver Head Lodge, seen below, which hosted thousands of guests through the years. His stories delighted all, including one where he lassoed a mountain lion and brought it back alive. In the photograph at left, Burk is presumably dressed for his guests. He was a member of the Arizona Game Protective Association and winner of the Arizona Big Ten Game Award. A set of Merriam's elk antlers that he found about 1920 hung over the front door of his Beaver Head Lodge. Burk's wife, Flora, was the first president of the Blue River Cowbelles, which first met in September 1954 at Beaver Head. (Both Trish Patterson; below, photograph by Homer L. Chaffee.)

Sprucedale Guest Ranch, located 14 miles south of Alpine at an elevation of 7,600 feet, has been owned and run by the Wiltbank family since 1941. That year, Walter Wiltbank bought the ranch for $9,000 at two-percent interest. Various historical buildings (for example, from the town of Maverick) have been brought to the ranch and refurbished for guests. Above, from left to right, ? Preston and Emer, Esther, Ellis, Fay, and Walter Wiltbank were photographed by guest Ross C. Preston. The image below was used for early advertising with the caption, "Meals are served in Sprucedale's spacious main lodge." Emer Wiltbank often took fishermen in to Wildcat Point. Today Sprucedale specializes in horseback riding but also provides other activities for their guests. (Both Emer and Esther Wiltbank.)

LOOKOUT POINT   BECKER BUTTE U.S. HY-60 ARIZONA
MEMORIAL TO GUSTAV BECKER OF SPRINGERVILLE

By 1930, the Arizona State Highway Department began planning a new route from Springerville to Globe through lower elevations, which meant less winter snow. This is the current route through Salt River Canyon, which upon completion was designated U.S. Highway 60. The efforts of Gustav Becker (and his son Julius) in establishing good, paved roads was recognized when a towering mesa in Salt River Canyon was named Becker Butte (above, left) and an overlook was created for sightseers. The dedication plaque called Gus Becker "A Father of U.S. Highway 60" and stated of Gus and Julius, "They made our World a better place in which to live." Other supporters of Highway 60 who attended the 1964 dedication (left) were, from left to right, David Campbell, William Huso, and William Sullivan. (Above, Fidencio Baca; at left, Mike Huso.)

Five

GATEWAY TO THE WHITE MOUNTAINS

Often described as a wonderland of scenic beauty, the rugged White Mountains of Arizona are a unique geographical treasure. Many acres fall within the boundaries of the Apache-Sitgreaves National Forests, where they are maintained as primitive wilderness. Featuring diverse plant and wildlife populations, the region's lush meadows and thick forests have supported a variety of industries, including logging, livestock grazing, and agriculture. Still rugged and relatively untamed, the highest peak within the White Mountains is Mount Baldy. Rising over 11,000 feet, the summit lies within the boundaries of the White Mountain Apache tribal lands. Some claim the range derived its name from the fact that its mountain summits frequently remained snowcapped for as many as seven months of the year.

This region offers year-round activities to locals, tourists, nature lovers, and outdoor enthusiasts. White Mountain fishing means trout—rainbow, German brown, and cutthroat. Nearby fish hatcheries require 18 to 24 months to produce trout for the fisherman. Native Arizona (Apache) trout have suffered from hybridization and competition with exotic species. With cattle grazing along creek banks, streams become wider, shallower, and warmer, and therefore less hospitable to the Apache trout. Today grazing along some streams is being controlled to ensure survival of the species.

In the 1960s, angleworms were a big business for White Mountain children, especially in Eagar. Signs in front yards read, "Large Worms," "Fresh Worms," "Worms While You Wait," and "Wiggly Worms." The most enterprising, however, may have been self-service, pre-packaged worms with the price clearly marked and a sign stating, "Thou Shalt Not Steal." For a period of time around 2000, worm races were held every July behind Ye Olde Tavern in Alpine. Each worm was placed in the center of a painted ring and given two minutes to crawl. The event could become heated with owners urging the potential fish bait on with squirts of water or shouts of encouragement. According to one account, early races included a "Robin," or person designated to dispose of the losing worms between shots of tequila.

The fourth Becker store, seen above, was in downtown Springerville; Gustav Becker continually made improvements. The most ambitious renovation was contracted to Bryant Whiting in 1950. Becker wanted 12-inch adobe walls replaced by modern brick, a new roof, new floors, and a complete basement. This was to be built "around, over, and under" the old building without closing the store for even one day. The basement proved particularly difficult, because solid rock required blasting. The entire building was jacked up, and two-foot I-beams were inserted. Then a low-profile caterpillar was located to push the dirt and rock from the basement out into trucks. After retirement, Whiting was president of the LDS temple in Mesa during its remodeling. He is pictured at left (center) in 1975 at the rededication with counselors Egbert Brown (left) and Elmer Gerber. (Above, ACHS/St. Johns; at left, Utah State Historical Society C-330.37.)

These two street scenes show Springerville in the early 20th century. Above is West Main Street, called "Chinatown," with the Chevrolet garage, El Paso-Grand Canyon Garage, Apache Theatre, and Sam's Club Café (owned by Sam Madariaga) pictured from left to right. Note that even at this early date, Springerville was called "Gateway to the White Mountains." Below is another photograph of Main Street, at a slightly later date, with the most prominent building being the Apache Chief Hotel. This building included a coffee shop, barbershop, and the early Western Drug. Both Conoco and 76 brand gasoline were sold at the end of the street. "Quality Meats" and "Quality Cleaners" are advertised on the left; the Madonna and two cafés are on the right. (Above, Trish Patterson; below, Fidencio Baca.)

Members of the Homrighausen, Becker, Rudd, Murray, Colter, Harper, Woods, Sharp, Snow, and Saffell families met in 1894 to form the First Presbyterian (Community) Church. Earlier a Sunday school was organized with Ernest Franz as superintendent. The new church had visiting pastors but no regular minister. Church outings included picnics at Becker Lake, swimming, fishing, marshmallow roasts, potlucks, and box suppers. The Ladies Aid Society was organized in 1915. (Ellis collection.)

On June 1, 1938, a new $105,000 federal building was dedicated in Springerville, perhaps the smallest community in the United States to have such a structure. Tazewell H. Lamb reported that an "eastern tourist in Springerville on dedication day stared across a green lawn at the two-storied concrete structure and turned to his wife [saying]: 'They'll be building 'em in cow pastures next.' " (Apache-Sitgreaves.)

Walter Wiltbank, at right, and Fay Ashcroft were married in 1932 and, like many other Mormon men of the time, Walter left soon afterward on a proselytizing mission. He served in the western states of Wyoming, New Mexico, and Colorado. Below is the remodel ground-breaking, with visiting church leader Oscar A. Kirkham handling the shovel, of the Eagar Ward LDS Church on February 20, 1948. Many of the area children are in the left side of the photograph. The men kneeling in front, from left to right, are W. B. Eagar, Albert Anderson, Bryant Whiting (with architectural plans), Ether Brown, Milford Hall, and Milo Wiltbank; standing next to Milo Wiltbank, from left to right, are Oscar Wilkins, Dan Burk, Emmett Reynolds, and Oscar Hamblin. From 1948 to 1951, additions were made to this early chapel; it was torn down in the 1980s and the current building was constructed. (At right, Emer Wiltbank; below, WMHS/Phelps Wilkins.)

People generally came to see World War I as a useless war. Although the United States came late into the war, most young men ages 21 to 30 were drafted. Above, Jesse Burk (left) is photographed with other men of his company. At left is Tomas Baca. Although a few men were given deferments for dependents, Baca left both a wife and child behind in Springerville. Upon his return, a large celebration was held, and Senito Gonzales finished his welcoming address with, "I was always satisfied that when our daring boys would get to France, they would be a credit to the U.S. and to Arizona, and especially to Apache County." (Above, Trish Patterson; at left, Fidencio Baca.)

After World War I, many American Legion posts were named after local men who had been killed in the war. Southern Apache County had four men who died in World War I: Andres Mascareño and John H. Slaughter of Springerville and Richard Judd and Sidney Severens of Alpine. Severens was originally from California, and his mother was the only one of the four to go on the 1930s Mother's Pilgrimage to France. The American Legion post was named after Slaughter (above), and presumably the men lined up in front of the building are all World War I veterans. The post erected the bronze plaque above a large piece of petrified wood (right) listing the names of the four who died. Of these four, Slaughter was probably the only one killed in action. (Above, Trish Patterson; at right, Fidencio Baca.)

Airplanes occasionally came to northeastern Arizona after World War I. These barnstorming pilots were itinerant air gypsies, always ready to demonstrate tailspins and other fancy maneuvers or give interested locals a bird's-eye view of their town. Shown above, possibly in November 1921 as mentioned in the *Holbrook News*, is Gustav Becker (right) with an unknown pilot. Becker family lore states that, upon takeoff, the wheel hit a prairie dog hole, the plane tipped, and the wooden propeller was cracked. By 1934, Becker was corresponding with C. E. Griggs, a federal airport engineer in Phoenix, about building an airfield for Springerville. Griggs wrote, "We will need a landing field 5200 feet in length, and 500 feet wide with the prevailing wind." The resulting airport is shown below. (Above, WHMS/Pat Christiansen; below, Ellis collection.)

Arizona water cannot be discussed without mentioning Fred T. Colter (right). Born in Nutrioso in 1879, he lived in New Mexico and then returned to Springerville to develop better irrigation for Apache County, including six reservoirs. (Below, a Forest Service truck adds a load of dirt to the Crescent Lake Dam in 1934.) He was a member of the state Constitutional Convention, elected to the legislature, and unsuccessfully ran for governor. In 1922, Arizona was asked to ratify the Colorado Compact dividing Colorado River water. Colter single-handedly led the fight using the slogan, "Save the Colorado for Arizona." He planned canals that would divert Colorado River water to central Arizona and fought water issues for 20 years, spending his entire fortune. After his death, U.S. Supreme Court decisions and the Central Arizona Project vindicated his ideas. (At right, WMHS; below, Apache-Sitgreaves.)

Clarcia Ashcroft was born in Ramah, New Mexico, and came to Eagar in 1927 with her siblings and widowed mother. She married Arthur Eagar and taught school for 40 years. She felt privileged to have met Robert Frost, Elmer Rice, Eleanor Roosevelt, Jesse Stuart, Carl Sandburg, David Brinkley, four Arizona governors, and two LDS Church presidents throughout the course of her life. She was also committed to the preservation of Apache County history. (Emer Wiltbank.)

Early schools were also used as community centers. Some buildings were too small to accommodate everyone who wanted to dance, so the people danced by numbers (with a little illegal trading). Occasionally dancers were divided by bare feet and boots, "an eminently sensible arrangement," wrote Clarcia Eagar. This 1923 Eagar class includes, from left to right, (front row) Teofilo ?, Kate Hoffman, Ethel Norton, Florenzio Hill, Madge Hale, Zora Hale, and Teofilo's brother; (second row) Gilbert Norton, Fred Martin, Earl Hale, Lorenzo Hill, Pearl Norton, Edith Martin (teacher), Lena Hale, Leonard ?, unidentified, unidentified. (Iris Finch.)

The third/fourth grade Springerville class, pictured with their teacher in October 1933, included, from left to right, (first row) Loween Silva, Carmela Chavez, Beverly Williams, Teresa Gonzales, Helen Nelson, Cleo Madareaga, Dorothy Cosper, Lura Childress, Katy Pipkins, and Julia Baca; (second row) Bertha Wahl, Maxine Miller, Mary Lindley, Julia Candelaria, Lucy Trammell, Juanita Bordeaux, Caroline Day, Dorothy Beard, Alice Metzler, and Amelia Voight; (third row) Irene Brinkmeyer (teacher), Franklin Miller, Paul Carillo, Roberto Torrez, James Hale, Tommy Baca, Robert Vaughn, Willie Chavez, Pete Candelaria, Arthur Romero, James Trammell, and Phil Silva Jr.; (fourth row) Lot Candelaria, Antonio Savaadra, Ray Moya, Richard Childress, Manuel Guiterrez, and Aurelio Najar. (WMHS.)

This school in Springerville originally had a bell. The bell is now on the lawn, and the school is being renovated for museum use. (Apache-Sitgreaves.)

Maverick, 40 miles south and over the mountain, was part of the Eagar District. With only a few children living in Maverick year round, the school had only two rooms. This 1948 photograph includes Denny Poer, Allen Odom, Norma O'Donnell, Billy Jo Chambers, Bobby Nilson, Clyde Mouser, JoAnne Odom, Jean Crunk, Dennis Chambers, and other unidentified children. When the logging camp was closed, the building was moved to Eagar. (Keith Eagar.)

Early high school students either attended the LDS academy at St. Johns or boarded in California or New Mexico. In 1921, a high school opened in Round Valley; the first class of eight girls graduated in 1923. Above is an early football team with coach Joe Jarvis (first row, right). By 1937, high school athletics included both football (no games won) and basketball (games won at Gallup, St. Johns, and Quemado). The girls were organized into a pep club, seen below. Morris Udall from St. Johns remembered that, in 1939, "during the last football game of the season when St. Johns played Round Valley I had to run off the field (I was the quarterback), drop my helmet, and pick up my trumpet to join the band for half-time entertainment. I thought nothing of it, because this was typical of the way school activities were organized." (Above, Trish Patterson; below, Aurora Eagar.)

High school activities in 1937 included a play called *The Outlaw King*, seen above, with Larry Burgess as Robin Hood, Jack Wiltbank as Friar Tuck, and Lot Burk as Little John. Pictured below, the school orchestra included, from left to right, (first row) Thayla Burgess, Verla Adair, Cleo Cosper, Marjorie Feaster, and Jerry Colter; (second row) Lula Eagar, Zelma Ashcroft, Karl Butler, Valora Butler, Frances Thompson, and Larry Burgess; (third row) Roberta Eagar, Della Crosby, Evelyn Bragg, Lamar Hamblin, Lydia Wiltbank, and C. Larson (teacher). The first annual was published in 1926–1927 as *The Apache*; later the yearbook was named *The Elk* and the school mascot also became an elk. (Both Aurora Eagar.)

Pictured from left to right, Freda Wiltbank, Nellie Hale, Idella Wiltbank, Mildred Norton, Isabell Norton, and Verena Wiltbank are standing with their dolls on the steps of the Amity school in 1917 or 1918. Ethel Coleman told of a Christmas when her mother said that Santa was too poor to bring a new doll, but he would put a new dress on it, "which he did much to my delight." (Iris Finch.)

Lucy Baca (left) and her sister Inez were small when their mother died, and they came to live with their grandmother Cruz Baca. Lucy described her grandmother as old-fashioned and strict but caring. The girls learned to help around the house, including washing with a washboard and bringing in wood and water. They were also sent to check on community members in case someone was sick or needed help. (Trish Patterson.)

Boy Scout troops were generally sponsored by local churches. In 1930, the Presbyterian church sponsored a troop; in 1939, they also added a Campfire Girls program. The Scout troop at left is ready for a trip to Mount Baldy in the summer of 1955 with scoutmaster Art Eagar. From left to right are (first row) Earl Burk, Tony Turley, Hank Gibson, Larry Slade, Chuck Martin, Terry Eagar, and Ellis Hamblin; (second row) Lyn Woods, Phelps Wilkins, and John Gibson. Below is Boy Scout Rush Norton in uniform about 1957. (At left, Terry and Lorene Eagar; below, Rush Norton.)

Joy is not usually a name given to a boy (except in northeastern Arizona). Pictured here is Joy Rencher about 1930 as he graduated from high school. Thomas Rencher and Camelia Jensen of Springerville/Eagar were married in 1903. In 1909, their two small children, Laura and Bernard, age five and three, died 12 days apart from scarlet fever. To this sad home came another son (whom they named Joy) and a daughter, Idona. (Keith Eagar.)

Lloyd Ashcroft, seen here, represents all from Apache County who served in the military during World War II. Many families sent several sons. George Crosby, John C. Hall, Joe Pearce, and Lee Wilhelm each had five children who served; William Lund and Charles Whiting had six sons. Wallace Hall and Armond Pearce carried Jimmy Slade at the end of the Bataan Death March, only to have Slade die when a Japanese prison ship was sunk. (Emer Wiltbank.)

Dancing was always important in the White Mountains. Even the first Catholic church at Springerville, seen above, was used for dances. Most dances had floor managers. If cowboys got too rowdy, the floor manager would give a signal the dance was over, and all would quietly file out. The band below was organized by a Mr. Aucherman, the music teacher in Round Valley in 1947–1948, and included, from left to right, Aucherman, Bud Merrill, Ardell Hale, Jack Udall, and Benjamin Slade. (Both Nadine Trickey.)

Milo Wiltbank's poetry was written for the people of his beloved White Mountains. Born in 1902 in Eagar, he memorialized kinfolk, neighbors, ranching, the mountains, and his personal work ethic. His historic ties are illustrated in this stanza: "Old wagon wheel, you've had your day / A changing world put you away / The noisy monsters of power and steel / Have taken your place, old wagon wheel." (Homer Rogers.)

This 1934 Ford V-8 on the Vernon road belonged to brothers Roy and Marion Wilhelm. The White Mountains are known for winter recreation, including skiing at Sunrise Park Resort. Owned by the White Mountain Apache Nation, the resort offers 800 acres of ski terrain, with 65 downhill ski runs on three mountains. Other outdoor recreation opportunities include ice fishing, tubing, cross-country skiing, sledding, snowboarding, and snowmobiling. (Mabel Wilhelm.)

In an effort to minimize damage to the forest floor during logging, the U.S. Forest Service sought out a contractor in the 1990s, trying to removing selected trees at KP Cienega using historical logging techniques—meaning horses. This proved to be a slow process, but the grass returned quickly, leaving little evidence of logging except the stumps. Today the same result is achieved with rubber-tire vehicles, and the process is much less time consuming. (Both Apache-Sitgreaves.)

In 1988, Val Kilmer (at right, far right) starred in Gore Vidal's *Billy the Kid*, a made-for-television movie for Turner Home Movies. The psychological Western premiered on the TNT network on May 10 the following year. For the production, Emer Wiltbank trucked the necessary horses from his White Mountain ranch to Old Tucson Studio locations (below). Kilmer lived in New Mexico for a time and felt a connection to the young outlaw. (Both Emer and Esther Wiltbank.)

Becker Lake has been used for regattas, fishing, ice-skating, and bird watching. Recreational use of the area increased in 2009 with the installation of a bridge over the Little Colorado River. Above, Phelps Wilkins cuts the ribbon. From left to right below are Jack Hustead, unidentified, Brian Crawford of the Arizona Game and Fish Department, and Bob and Kay Dison standing on the completed bridge. Now a River Walk is available for everyone to enjoy. (Both Phelps Wilkins.)

In the Territory of Arizona, Merriam's elk were hunted to extinction by about 1900. Then, through the efforts of Dr. Robert N. Looney and money raised by Elks lodges, elk from Yellowstone National Park were shipped to Arizona in 1914 and released south of Winslow. Other releases were made during the 1920s; the last release was on February 12, 1927, at Campbell Blue on the Coronado Trail. (Arizona Game and Fish Department, photograph by George Andrejko.)

With a 1997 press conference in the fireplace room of Hannagan Meadow Lodge, Secretary of the Interior Bruce Babbitt announced a reintroduction program for the Mexican gray wolf. Once considered a threat to the livestock industry, bounty was paid until they were gone in the 1940s. With the Endangered Species Act of 1973, a captive rearing program began, and 11 wolves were introduced into the Blue Range Recovery Area in March 1998. (Hannagan Meadow Lodge.)

The huge Rodeo-Chediski fire of 2002 eventually encompassed more than 460,000 acres. Thousands of area residents from Heber to Show Low were displaced, and many private homes were opened to accept friends and relatives. As evacuated homeowners streamed into Round Valley, some were housed in the high school sports arena (above). The arena is the area's most iconic landmark and is variously referred to as the Dome, the Round Valley Ensphere, the "damn Dome," or "that huge pink monstrosity." A week after the fire began, Pres. George W. Bush visited (below), offering words of encouragement to firefighters and displaced families. (Both Apache-Sitgreaves.)

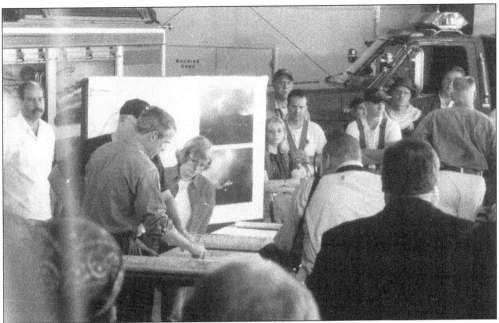

With President Bush's visit, the Rodeo-Chediski fire area was declared a federal disaster area, allowing residents to apply for relief funds to repair or replace damaged homes. Above, President Bush confers with Gov. Jane Hull and area firefighters; below, news media from around the state provide updates to Arizona residents wanting information about their summer properties or news about homes and businesses owned by family and friends. With major arteries from the White Mountains into Phoenix closed by the fire, Fox News evidently found it more convenient to send a crew from Henderson/Las Vegas, Nevada, than from Phoenix. (Both Apache-Sitgreaves.)

In 1951, the Becker family celebrated 75 years of mercantile activities in Arizona. Barry Goldwater poses here with the *Apache County Independent News* reporting this milestone. A year later, Goldwater would be elected to the U.S. Senate and represent Arizona for five terms. (AHS/Tucson Becker collection.)

Jack Becker (left) and his uncle Gustav Edward "Gus" Becker are looking over the old Becker store registers on July 13, 1994. Jack helped preserve his family's history and, more importantly, spent countless hours researching the beginnings of Springerville/Eagar before his untimely death in 2007. Some of this research, particularly from early Arizona and New Mexico newspapers, is available at www.roundvalleyaz.com. (Carol Becker.)

In July 2009, the Forest Service announced, "For the first time in history, Arizona has been invited to provide the United States Congress with the Capitol Christmas tree. Placed in front of the Capitol building, *Arizona's Gift From the Grand Canyon State* will be a 75 ft. conifer tree selected from the Apache-Sitgreaves National Forests. Found in the White Mountains of northeastern Arizona, the tree will travel throughout Arizona and across the nation to its place of honor. The iconic symbol of the holidays will be lit during a ceremony by the Speaker of the House, along with an Arizona school child who has made an ornament for the tree." Christmas trees from the White Mountains have graced living rooms throughout Arizona; now a tree from Arizona has been displayed on the U.S. Capitol grounds. Pictured below are the children of Rickey and Deanna Turner and Spencer and Heather Rosenbaum. These sixth-generation Arizonans, now living in Manhattan, New York, and Washington, D.C., celebrated their heritage by bringing their children to visit to the capitol's Christmas tree from the White Mountains. (Both photographs by Jared Ellis.)

Visit us at
arcadiapublishing.com